Captain Comet
and the
Purple Planet

Jonathan Emmett

Illustrated by Andy Parker

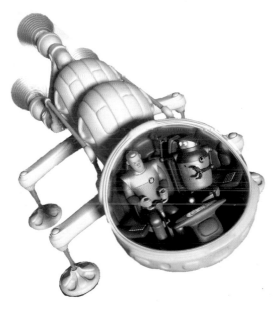

1

Spanner is bored

It was a quiet morning at Stardust Space Station. Captain Stella was checking the space shuttle.

Captain Comet was watering the plants and Spanner the robot was bored.

'Can I sit at the control desk?' he asked.

'All right,' said Captain Comet, 'But don't touch anything and *don't* press that red button.'

Spanner sat down at the desk and looked at all the buttons.

There were buttons to open all the space station doors and buttons to turn on all the lights.

There was even a button to flush all the toilets!

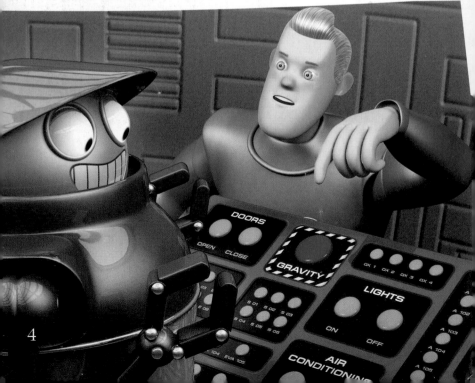

There was also a big red button, labelled 'Gravity'.

Spanner was not sure what 'Gravity' was.

'I'll press it very quickly,' said Spanner, 'to see what it does.'

He pressed the red button.

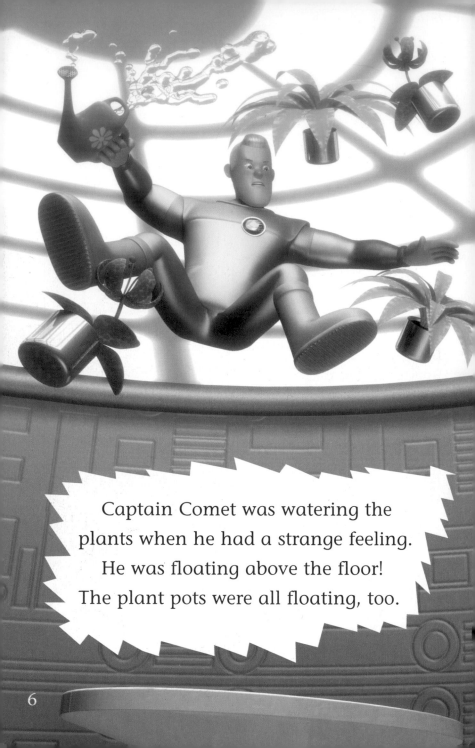

Captain Comet was watering the plants when he had a strange feeling. He was floating above the floor! The plant pots were all floating, too.

He guessed what had happened.

'Spanner!' he shouted, 'I told you not to touch that red button!'

Spanner saw that gravity was what made things stay on the floor.

There was no gravity in space, so the space station made its own.

Spanner pressed the red button to
make the gravity come back on again
– and all the pot plants fell to the floor.
Comet fell to the floor beside them.
'SPANNER!' Comet groaned.

SPLASH!

2

It must be a planet

Spanner was cleaning up the mess for the rest of the morning.

When he turned the cleaner off, everyone heard a beeping noise. The noise was coming from the space scanner.

Everyone stopped what they were doing and came to look.

'The scanner has found something,' said Comet.

He pointed to a flashing dot that was moving across the scanner screen.

'I wonder what it is?' said Captain Stella.

'Is it an asteroid?' asked Spanner. 'An asteroid is a lump of rock that floats in space.'

'I *know* that!' said Captain Comet. 'Anyway, it's too big to be an asteroid,'

'Then it must be a planet,' Spanner said.

'Where has it come from?' asked Comet. 'And why is it moving so fast?'

'You'd better go and have a look,' said Captain Stella.

Comet and Spanner set off in the
space shuttle to look for the new
planet. Spanner was very excited.

'I've never found a new planet
before,' he said. 'What shall we call it?'

'Let's find it first,' said Comet.

But Spanner wasn't listening. 'I'm going to call it *Planet Spanner*,' he said.

Spanner made a humming noise and a flag came out of a slot in his chest.

'What **are** you doing?' asked Comet.

'I've made a flag to put on *Planet Spanner.* Then everyone will know that we were the first to find it,' Spanner explained.

He showed Comet the flag. It was bright red with two spanners on it.

Comet had to smile. 'Very nice,' he said.

3

On the Purple Planet

The planet looked very strange. It was purple and covered in huge spikes.

Comet landed the shuttle carefully on the planet.

Then he got out to have a look around.

Spanner stayed in the shuttle, making a flagpole for his flag.

Spanner found a
metal rod.

He fastened the
flag to one end of the rod
and put the other end into
a hole in his chest.

There was a
noise like an
electric pencil
sharpener. When
he took the
rod out
again, it had
a nice sharp point.

Comet was looking at one of the giant purple spikes. It felt soft and warm.

'That's very odd,' thought Comet. 'This spike feels like it's alive.'

Just then Spanner arrived with his new flagpole. 'I name this planet – *Planet Spanner!*' he said proudly.

'No! STOP!' Comet yelled.

But before Comet could stop him,
Spanner hammered the sharp flagpole
into the ground.

There was a huge roar.

'What was *that?*' asked Spanner.

'Quick, back to the shuttle!' shouted
Comet, as the ground began to shake.

They strapped themselves into their seats and Comet blasted off.

Spanner looked at the screen. The planet's surface was spinning around.

Then the opening of a big, dark cave came into view.

Around the outside of the opening were large, jagged rocks.

'Look! ' said Spanner. 'They're like giant teeth!'

Comet stared at the screen.

'That's because they ARE giant teeth!' he said, as two huge, angry eyes came into view.

'It's not a planet...' said Comet,

'... It's a SPACE MONSTER!' gasped Spanner.

4
Space Chase

'Why is it so angry with us?'
cried Spanner.

'You've just hammered a big sharp
flagpole into its backside,' explained
Captain Comet.

The huge teeth snapped shut behind
them. 'It wants to eat us!' wailed
Spanner. 'We've got to get away!"

'That's what I'm *trying* to do!'
said Comet. 'But it's too fast!'

Comet fired the shuttle's jets.
Then he tried to make a sharp turn,
as the monster zoomed towards them.

'What are we going to do?'
cried Spanner.

Just then, Captain Stella's face appeared on the screen. She had been watching them on the space scanner.

Captain Comet tried to make another sharp turn. The space monster was getting closer and closer.

'Are you all right?' Captain Stella asked. 'What's going on?'

'WE'RE GOING TO BE EATEN!'
wailed Spanner. 'BY A PRICKLY PURPLE
SPACE MONSTER THE SIZE OF A
PLANET!'

'Apart from that, everything's fine,'
said Comet, making the shuttle dive to
dodge the giant teeth.

'Can I help?" asked Captain Stella.

'No,' said Comet. 'You're too far away. Is there anyone closer?'

Stella looked at the space map and shook her head.

'No, there are no space stations or planets – only asteroids,' she said.

'Asteroids!' Comet said. 'Tell me where they are. I've got an idea!'

5

Into the Asteroids

The space shuttle zoomed towards the asteroids.

Spanner and Comet had never been so close to the asteroids before.

Some of the asteroids were as big as office blocks.

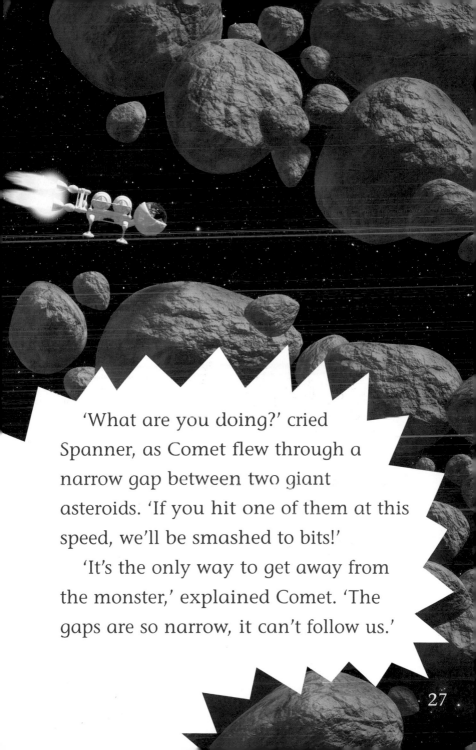

'What are you doing?' cried
Spanner, as Comet flew through a
narrow gap between two giant
asteroids. 'If you hit one of them at this
speed, we'll be smashed to bits!'

'It's the only way to get away from
the monster,' explained Comet. 'The
gaps are so narrow, it can't follow us.'

Comet was right. The space monster stopped chasing them. Then it flew up to an asteroid – and took a big bite out of it.

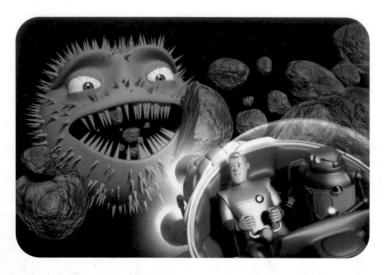

Comet and Spanner watched as the monster chomped its way happily through two or three asteroids.

'It eats asteroids!' Spanner said.

'I'm glad it didn't eat US!' Comet smiled.

'We didn't find a new planet after all,' grumbled Spanner, on the way back to the space station.

'No,' said Comet. 'But we did find a new kind of space monster.'

'That's true,' said Spanner. 'But how will anyone know that we were the first to find it?'

Captain Comet took one last look at the purple monster and smiled.

'Oh, they'll know. After all, it does have YOUR FLAG sticking out of its bottom!' he said.

About the Author

I've always loved space adventures, but this is the first one that I've written myself.

The idea for the planet monster came from a photograph of a purple porcupine fish. When it's in danger, this fish puffs up its body into a big spiky ball and looks just like the monster in the story.

You can find out more about Jonathan Emmett's books by visiting his website at www.scribblestreet.co.uk